HACKING

A Quick and Simple Introduction to the Basics of Hacking, Scripting, Cybersecurity, Networking, and System Penetration

HANS WEBER

Table of Contents

Introduction

If you ask someone what hacking is, they will typically tell you that it is someone that penetrates the security of a system and gains access to it. That is surprisingly not what it always meant. The word "Hacker" was initially used to refer to anyone that was a skilled programmer, but due to popular cultural representations, the definitions have changed over time. So let us dig deeper into some basics of hacking and try to explain the culture, the misunderstandings, and the technicalities.

What is a Security Hacker?

When we refer to a hacker, we are typically talking about a security hacker. A security hacker is a person who can exploit an existing computer or network system and is able to use it for their personal motives. To further understand the motives of hackers, we have to look into the different types of hackers that exist and how they use the information or power that they gain once they have accessed a system.

The Different Kinds of Hackers:

Among the many kinds of hackers that exist, there are three that are popularly depicted through the media and are popularly referred to. They are as follows:

1. **Black hat hacker**: A hacker who has malicious intent

2. **Grey hat hacker**: A hacker who has good intent but hacks without seeking permission

3. **White hat hacker**: A hacker with a good intent that seeks permission before hacking

We will be looking at each of the classifications in detail in further chapters.

Other Classifications of Hackers

There are other ways that security hackers are classified. These include classifications by the skills of a hacker. Some of the following are commonly used skill-based classifications:

1. **Elite Hacker:** The most skilled hacker having extensively exploited systems

2. **Script Kiddie:** A hacker that lacks experience and uses pre-written scripts

3. **Neophyte (Newbie/Noob):** A hacker who lacks both knowledge and experience

How Does a Hacker Hack into a System?

When hacking into a system, a hacker follows a number of steps to ensure that they can enter and use the system as they require. These can be broadly categorized into three separate subheadings, which are as follows:

1) **Network Enumeration/Reconnaissance:** Network enumeration is the first step of hacking. It involves getting acquainted with the system and networks that the victim is using. This usually involves retrieving sensitive data about the network, including the usernames and information of members that use the network, as well as their

email addresses. A hacker typically downloads the entire website. Overt discovery protocols are used for this step of the procedure.

2) **Vulnerability Analysis:** After having carried out a network enumeration, the hacker now knows the people and entities that are a part of a network. The next step is to find the vulnerabilities within the systems that are connected to the network. This allows the hacker to enter the network by exploiting the vulnerabilities that he may have found. Many tools, such as vulnerability or a port scanner, exist to allow a hacker to analyze vulnerabilities within a system quickly. A hacker may also manually test vulnerabilities by looking for automated emails and the email server that is being used by the staff.

3) **Exploitation:** The final step of hacking comes in the form of exploitation. Exploitation refers to overpowering the vulnerabilities to make the software or network act in an inconsistent manner. This is typically the stage that most people refer to as "hacking," and we will look into it in extensive detail when we discuss cybersecurity.

After having actively hacked into a network, a hacker tries to maintain a low profile. They can do so by accessing accounts that have not been used for a long time, or making an admin account for themselves and trying to blend in. Hackers also typically attack after having changed their IPs and machine codes to ensure that there is no track of their activity left. If no one notices the new staff member on the site, the hacker has successfully blended in and can continue to do as they wish on the site. That is why it is important to keep track of your staff members and ensure that they aren't "ghost" members.

How to Keep your Network Safe

Now that we know how a hacker manages to access a system or a network, we can logically conclude ways to ensure that the hacker is unable to get into it. The first one is obviously to ensure that your staff members aren't traceable, and vulnerabilities don't exist within the website or network that you run. Unfortunately, that is not as easy as it sounds, and vulnerabilities continue to pop up in all sorts of networks. This includes high-profile tech companies, including Apple and Facebook. That is why it is important always to ensure that you have the updated version of the apps. Updates typically exist to resolve security issues or other bugs.

So you might be wondering, if big-tech firms like those are unable to keep themselves safe, how could you? Well, the answer is pretty simple. While it may not be possible to close off all vulnerabilities, it is possible to train your staff. Ensure that you keep a good check on the members of your network, immediately see the history of any anomalies and take action, and train your staff never to leave their emails vulnerable or ghost accounts standing without informing the management of the network. That way, you will be able to ensure that no hacker manages to exploit any vulnerability that they may find, and all threats are promptly taken care of.

What Can Be Hacked?

It is a common misconception that only systems such as computers can be hacked, and everything else is typically safe. The fact is that anything and everything that is connected to a network can be hacked by exploiting the network itself. While a complete list would be exhaustive, some of the things that can be hacked include baby monitors, smart TVs, thermostats, printers, and cameras. In a now-famous incident, someone hacked into 50,000 printers and made them rapidly print out messages asking people to subscribe to Pewdiepie.

Can a Network be Un-Hackable?

While there are a number of ways to make your network secure enough to deter hackers from trying to enter it, there are no websites or networks that can prove to be unhackable. Even secure networks such as the NSA have been hacked at one point or another. A popular Reddit thread lists all games that call themselves "unhackable," followed by a general challenge to hack them. All of them eventually got hacked.

Chapter One

Black Hat Hacking

Now that we know the basics of hacking well, we can dig deeper into the motives of certain types of hackers and what they aim to do by making their way into a system. Any such list obviously starts with the black hat hackers, popularly depicted as villainous typists that work on a black screen, by media.

Motives of Black hat Hackers

To understand the operations of such hackers, it is important that we understand the motives that they have when trying to hack into a system. The motives are usually broadly tagged as personal gain but can be categorized into a number of classes. Typical motives can include the follows:

1) **Blackmailing:** While blackmailing is not an ultimate motive, it is usually what encourages a hacker to hack into the data. By getting access to the data, they are able to blackmail the owner and gain personal benefits. These include financial gains as well as making the person being blackmailed oblige to a request.

2) **Financial gains:** Financial gains can be achieved in a number of ways by black hat hacking. We have already discussed that people can be blackmailed to get money. Other ways of gaining financially include selling the personal that the hacker manages to steal, and

working for a third party and getting paid for the hacking services. Hackers can also hack directly into your bank account and take your funds!

3) **Revenge/Fun:** While typically not the motive of skilled hackers, novice hackers may hack into the data of a person simply for fun, or for some form of revenge.

4) **To practice hacking:** A typical black hacker that is still learning may hack into a website and make it unusable simply for practice, to enable themselves to target bigger and more secure networks in the future.

The Harm of Black hat Hacking

There are a number of harms that we are exposed to when we are targeted by black hat hacking. Contrary to their white hat alters, black hat hackers typically lack moral responsibility and thus take little to no care of how the data that they are hacking is being used.

This means that while a hacker may have hacked the data for an entirely different purpose, having gained access to it, they might just leak it to the internet. Marketplaces in the dark web typically buy such data, making it public knowledge. In a recent attack, someone leaked 773 million emails and 21 million passwords online. With breaches at this massive scale, we should ensure that we keep our passwords secure so that no one can gain unauthorized access to our accounts.

Other than leaking your data online and allowing anyone access to your account, there are other harms that come with black hat hacking. The first of these would be a financial loss. In the case of being blackmailed, you might choose to pay money against having your privacy being compromised. By hacking into your bank data, they can also easily transfer funds from your account into their own, and thus rip you of your money.

Black hat hacking is particularly dangerous for those who run servers or networks. A black hat hacker would have little care when trying to enter a vulnerable system and can thus use extreme methods to ensure that they get control. That not only means that they might render your site or network useless for the time, but also that they might take over the ownership of the site and use it as they wish, stealing yours, your staff's and your customer's data. That is why it is important that any attempts at hacking are promptly dealt with, and security is tight enough to discourage any hackers.

The Legality of Black hat Hacking

Hacking itself is not illegal. That is because there are a number of ways in which hacking can promote good within society. However, given the work that black hat hackers do, their hacking being non-consensual, their operations are illegal. While laws greatly vary with country, depending on the severity of the case, black hat hackers may find themselves facing years of jail time and thousands of dollars in fine, as well as payment for any damages, caused. We have seen some cases where hackers have received as many as 90 years of jail time.

Chapter Two

White Hat Hacking

In contrast to the black hat hackers that seek to exploit vulnerabilities of a system for personal gains and break laws in doing so, white hat hackers follow the laws and hack only with consent. That does not, however, mean that the hacking itself is not for their personal gains. Let us explore how these ethical hackers operate and what their motives are.

Why do White hat Hackers Exist?

White hat hackers surprisingly exist because black hat hackers do. If there were no black hat hackers, no white hat hackers would be needed to check the system for flaws and vulnerabilities. White hat hackers primarily get the consent from a network admin and try tap or hack into their network. If they are successfully able to do so, they tell the vulnerabilities within the network to the admin and may offer to help them close any such vulnerabilities. The role of the white hat hacker is the exact opposite of the black hat hacker, and they aim to protect and secure a system. The methodologies that both kinds of hackers use are the same, though.

Motives of White hat Hackers

So you may be wondering why someone would want to hack into a system with consent to find vulnerabilities. There are a number of reasons that white hat hackers would do so, and we are going to list some of them below:

1) **Securing their Network:** Hackers are typically very skilled programmers and might own their own website or network. They might attack their own network with the motive of finding vulnerabilities and securing them, to ensure that no one else can gain unauthorized access into it.

2) **Financial Gains:** White hat hackers, particularly the good ones, are paid high by companies that wish for the flaws and vulnerabilities in their systems to be closed. Thus by being a white hat hacker, a person can earn a large amount of money through being paid for the services that they offer.

3) **Social Service:** A hacker might wish to provide a social service by raising awareness about data security. They could thus work with companies for free and show them their vulnerabilities.

4) **Learning:** A newbie hacker may offer their services for free in a bid to learn. If a white hat hacker is able to hack into a complicated and secure system, they are typically offered better payment packages earlier in their careers.

A typical white hat hacker can earn a lot more money than most careers have to offer. Many companies offer thousands of dollars for anyone to identify any vulnerability within their network and might offer more for that person to fix them.

Benefits of White hat Hackers

The benefits of having white hat hackers are many fold, and the most important one is to find vulnerabilities within a system. When a white hat hacker is able to identify the problems within a system, they are quickly fixed. This means that when a black hat hacker tries to hack into the system, he will find that the vulnerabilities no longer exist, and would thus be unable to do much damage.

In an ideal scenario, this should ensure that no black hat hacking occurs. However, there are a number of issues with that. First of all, not many networks hire white hat hackers. That means that they are left open to the vulnerabilities that exist within the system. To add to that, some black hat hackers may be more adept than a white hat hacker and may be able to find vulnerabilities that the ethical hacker missed out on, which means that the system is still open for flaws. That is why we should never let our guard down.

Earnings of a White hat Hacker

A white hat hacker can typically earn a median salary of over 80,000 dollars. Each assignment can earn anything from 15,000 to 20,000 dollars, and the best bounty hunters can manage to earn as much as 500,000 dollars a year.

The Legality of White hat Hackers

White hat hacking is legal, as it does not break any of the laws and is done with consent. White hat hacking is thus considered a reputable career and can bring you big earnings, and is legal on top of that. If one wants to learn hacking and system penetration, they should try and go for a white hat hacker profession.

Chapter Three

Grey Hat Hacking

Laying between white hat and black hat hacking is grey hat hacking. While typically it was not recognized, it has now become a huge part of the hacking industry and is thus given more notice. Grey hat hacking is technically ethical hacking, and the person engaging in it has no malicious intent and does not intend to steal data or blackmail someone. They also, however, do not seek consent before engaging in the activity and are thus put in a "grey" spot between black and white hat hackers.

Why Would Someone Engage in Grey hat Hacking?

While the motives of most white hat and black hat hackers are clear cut, people in the grey area are harder to read. Nonetheless, there are a number of reasons that we can identify for which someone would want to engage in grey hat hacking.

1) **Financial Gain:** The primary reason that people engage in grey hat hacking is for financial gain. When being unable to find jobs as a white hat hacker, they typically hack into a vulnerable network and tell the company about it, seeking monetary rewards and to be hired to fix the vulnerability. Many companies now tend to report such activities, though, and that means that financial gains have minimalized.

2) **Learning:** When you're a hacker, the whole web is your platform. Learning hackers that wish to engage in ethical hacking in the future might feel that they need to learn by hacking into random sites. While no malicious intent exists on their part, it is still illegal. A number of sites now offer hackers to attempt to hack them for learning purposes, removing the need to learn using illegal means.

3) **Activism:** Perhaps the most widespread usage of grey hat hacking is for activism purposes. This type of hacking is now coined as red hat hacking. We will dedicate a separate section to exploring this form of hacking.

The Legality of Grey hat Hacking

Grey hat hacking is not legal. The legal implications are typically the same as those in the black hat hacking scenarios. However, given that most grey hat hackers do not seek to harm a site, and at times only wish to help, the incidents are typically not reported at a high rate, which means that grey hat hackers are not always punished. That tends to encourage the activities of such hackers.

The Curious Case of Kevin Mitnick

No story of grey hat hacking is complete without the mention of Kevin Metnick. Having started hacking into systems at a young age of 12, Kevin had managed to hack his way through many high-security systems, including Motorola, Netcom, and Nokia. He had over a hundred spoof cells and codes that he used to hide his location. He was soon listed as the most wanted hacker and subsequently sentenced to 5 years of jail time.

After having served jail time, Kevin turned over a new leaf and moved from grey to white hat hacking. He wrote multiple books, many of which went on to become bestsellers. He now works with many of the Fortune 500 companies and helps provide them with solutions to their vulnerabilities.

Kevin is now one of the best-known hackers in the world, and his story shows us that grey hat hacking, despite how safe it might seem, is not legal or encouraged. If you feel that you have a knack for hacking, you should go team white!

The Controversial Red Hat Hacking

Red hat hacking is currently branched under the umbrella of grey hat hacking. It is more popularly known as hacktivism and is a prime spotlight of the innovations to hacking in the 21st century.

Hacktivism is typically used as a form of activism, and the hacker uses hacking to draw public interest to a matter of global concern that should be taken note of immediately. Groups of hacktivists exist, including Anonymous.

One of the prime activities that Hacktivists have engaged in is the deletion of sites that display child porn. By gaining access to those sites and deleting their content, they have managed to clean the internet of illegal and immoral content.

WikiLeaks is a depository of documents that were obtained using hacktivism measures, including many state and national secrets that the hackers believe people have a right to know. As many as 400,000 documents about the US war on Iraq exist on the WikiLeaks server.

Hacktivism is typically illegal since it involves hacking into websites without consent, but it may be considered legal when the hackers hack the deep web to remove problematic content from it.

Chapter Four

Networks

No book about hacking is complete without a mention of networks. If a computer system or data is stored solely in a system with no network connected to it, the hacker would only be able to access it if they were able to access it physically. It is due to networks that hackers are able to enter a system and get access to the data.

What is a Network?

A network is a system in which different entities are connected together. A computer network is no different and consists of interconnected computers that share information with each other.

How are Networks Connected?

Networks are connected and made through a number of ways. Some networks may be connected to each other using the common copper wires that we see being used for the slower internet modems. Other networks are formed through the more solid fiber cables with faster connection speeds. Networks don't need to be hooked together at all and can be formed through all the devices connected to single Wi-Fi.

Types of Network

There are two broad types of networks. The first type is a Local area network, also known as a LAN. The LAN typically connects entities within a small distance and includes simple systems such as those in a company where all the systems are connected to one another. A simple benefit of using the LAN network would be better utilizing the resources. By using a LAN network in a company, you can make your job easier and save space.

How it works is that you would have one computer dedicated to storage. It would store all the files as well as all the software. The other systems can simply use the resources from the storage system, which means that the files and software do not need to be in every computer in the system.

The second type of network is the WAN network, also known as the Wide Area Network. This is a non-internalized network that connects one entity to outside entities. It thus connects all LANs to one another, letting them pass information between one another. The Internet is a WAN and connects almost all servers in the world in one way or another.

The internet does operate in a way similar to the LAN networks. All the files that you require are contained on the internet, which means that you don't have to go out and locally seek images, text, software, and information. However, access to the internet, or any network for that, does leave you vulnerable to the problems associated with hacking since someone can tap into your network and steal your data. This is why care needs to be taken with any network that is connected to a network in any way.

Are We Safe if We Never Connect to a Network?

While it is typically not a choice, given how everyone in today's world does need access to resources that you can get from the internet or other sources, let us assume that a computer was hypothetically speaking, never connected to a network. In that case, we would be safe only if the hacker cannot physically access the system. If the hacker is physically able to access the system, he would still be able to enter it using the methods that they typically use.

To demonstrate the point, we'll give you an example of something else that penetrates the system: a virus. The Stuxnet virus was made specifically to target uranium facilities in Iran. While the computers that ran the uranium centrifuges had no active internet connection and were not connected to any outside networks, the virus lay dormant in thousands of devices. Eventually, disaster struck as someone plugged a USB into the system. The dormant virus had affected the USB as well and thus managed to take control of the centrifuges and destroy Iran's uranium and thus nuclear program.

This example shows that the only way to ensure absolute safety is to ensure that the system is never connected to an outside source. With the world now at our fingertips, that definitely doesn't seem to be a viable option!

How does a Hacker Access a Network?

A hacker accesses a network using the steps that we already mentioned in the first chapter. They first find information about the network, then use the information to find vulnerabilities, and then use the vulnerabilities to exploit the system. For clarity purposes, we will give you an example.

Let's assume that there is a server that has 200 active users all logged into the system with access to the files. The hacker would first plan on getting the information on all the users and the system itself. Let's say the system is a website that produces daily content. The hacker would download the site and use a number of tools to analyze who uses the site and what their usernames and emails are.

Once the hacker has that information, he knows that he can now target the users to find a vulnerability in the network. To do this, he might try and crack the password of one of the old unused email accounts that are linked to the site and have access to the files.

After having managed to crack the password (and thus exploited the vulnerability), the hacker would then be into the system and can both get the data or delete it as he wishes. This is why networks are typically very dangerous, and there are a number of security measures employed to ensure that no one can exploit them.

If you have questions over how a hacker can exploit the vulnerability, or how a network is made or can be made secure, then continue reading because we will be digging into the details in the latter half of this book!

Chapter Five

Scripting and Other Tools

Before we dig into the ways that systems can be hacked into in detail, and explain how you can be protected against them, it is important that you know about scripting as well as other tools that hackers typically use. Scripting is one of the main tools in the arsenal of a hacker, and it helps them access the information quicker than they could have otherwise. That makes it important for hackers to be able to script when they are beginning to dig deeper into the world of hacking.

What is Scripting?

Scripting is a way of automating tasks that would otherwise have been had to be written down and coded individually. By running a script, you can basically let the machine do what you would have had to do otherwise. Scripts are typically written in the shell (The black box, so movies didn't get it all wrong!) The help that scripting provides when it comes to hacking is simple. Hackers have to analyze a lot of data to find vulnerabilities or try to exploit them. That would take thousands of lines of code, and mean that cracking into a site would simply not be feasible. With scripts, though, the job becomes way easier. The elite hackers typically make scripts that are used to dig through the system with ease, and with little human input.

What makes Scripts so Dangerous?

What makes scripts so dangerous is how easily available they are. Novice hackers, particularly Script kiddies, typically just use the script to gain access to hacking tools, and can cause DDoS attacks, which can harm companies and cause them thousands in revenue damages. Scripts made to code, or even test, can thus be disastrous in the wrong hands.

Some Script-Based Tools used for Ethical Hacking

Some script-based tools that you can easily find on the internet and use for ethical hacking include:

1) **John the Ripper:** An open-source tool that you can easily download. It is one of the most versatile password hackers and uses intelligent algorithms to decipher passwords based on the encryption of a system

2) **Metaspoilt:** This tool contains a number of scripts pre-written into it that can scan for and find vulnerabilities within any system, and help you exploit them.

3) **IronWasp:** A multiplatform tool that can search for as many as 25 different web vulnerabilities.

With these kinds of scripts being available for public use, the dangers to any small business sites are typically large. That is why it is recommended that you hire an ethical hacker or a programmer to ensure that all such mainstream vulnerabilities are closed off, and the system does not have to suffer as a consequence.

Is Hacking Easy?

Given that we just told you about a number of tools that can help you hack into systems, find vulnerabilities, and crack passwords, you must be wondering if hacking is easy. The answer to the question is somewhat complicated and mostly depends on a few factors.

If you plan to hack a small recently established site that does not use any security protocols and is completely unprotected, then yes, hacking would ultimately be easy. If, however, you're trying to crack the password of another person on Facebook, Jack the Ripper will be of no use to you. To work around those systems, you can't use pre-made widely available scripts since those vulnerabilities would already have been closed off. You would need to observe the code of the system instead, find any potential vulnerabilities, and custom-make a script to exploit it. So in those cases, hacking is definitely not easy, and we can see why ethical hackers are able to bag so much money.

In the later chapters, we will be discussing how hackers attack and how you can stop them from causing damage to you and your system.

Chapter Six

The Different Types of Hacking
and How they Work

Now that we know all about the basics of hacking, we will see how hacking actually works by looking into real-world examples and how they work. This will be an extensive list and should let you know about all the major ways that people can hack into your system or account. In the later chapters, we will also consider how you can protect yourself against all of these methods of hacking, and how systems have been made that work to protect you from them.

Physical Hacking

Perhaps the technique of hacking that we get to hear the least about is physical hacking. That is because, in today's world, physical access points are too secure for most people to be able to break through them. Nonetheless, it remains a valid technique for hacking and one that you need to secure yourself against.

Physical hacking involves physically gaining access to the data. This can be done using a number of methods. If you are a data center owner, hackers can typically climb in through the ceiling or through the air vents that are placed for cooling. Unless these places are carefully secured, they can easily grab the data that they require physically.

In cases of a company, hackers can typically masquerade an employee and enter the company, physically hacking into the system and easily being able to intercept and gain access to any data that they wish to.

Another way that a person can physically hack data is by tapping into the lines that connect you to the outside world. While it was much easier to do in the past, and a hacker could have managed to eavesdrop on your phone call had they access to the wire cord, now it has become an increasingly difficult task due to a number of reasons that we will discuss in the later chapters.

Brute Force

While being one of the most common attacks in the past, brute force is no longer used for a lot of websites. Nonetheless, for those that have not secured themselves, it remains a goldmine. A brute force hacking script works in a simple manner. It has a database to go with it that contains any and all possible combinations that could be used as a password on a website. That's trillions of entries!

The brute force command module then begins to enter the passwords one by one into the system. Each time a password is not accepted, it will move on to the next one until it is eventually able to find the correct password. Such an attack obviously takes time to execute, but given the power of computers today, it can be done relatively quickly.

Another innovation in the brute force technology is the usage of smarter scripts. The scripts now don't check every word on the list, but rather check only the passwords that would have been considered valid.

Let's consider that a certain website has the following requirements for the password:

- At least 8 characters in length
- At least one capitalized letter
- At least 1 number
- At least 1 symbol

In such a case, the newer and smarter Brute force script would not start from the typical list, but would rather make a specific list of all possible combinations given the conditions. The first item on the list could thus be @@@@@1aA.

Another improvement has come in the form of how the Brute force attacking module starts to input possible combinations. While initially, it used the list in alphabetical sequence, the program now runs the script to check for common passwords first, greatly shortening the time that it takes for a script to find a password.

Phishing

Phishing is a popular form of hacking, and one of the simplest ones for the hacker. Phishing attacks are now taking more sophisticated forms as well and might be given the name of Smishing. The basic concept of all these attacks is the same: the person that is trying to hack you pretends to be someone that you trust to get your information out of you. This can be done in a number of ways.

The first method comes in the form of appearing to be a website that they aren't. This is done by naming their website's name closely on the website that you actually wished to visit, i.e., facebo0k.com instead of facebook.com.

The second step comes in the form of getting people to visit the website. They might offer in-app advertising which would offer some promo and people might click it. Once people click on the ad, they are redirected to the fake website that the hacker has made. The URLs are pretty similar, and the website design is exactly the same. The coding is very different, though, and once someone enters the password into the fake website that the hacker has made, the password is saved in a database. Thus while people think that they entered information on a legit website, all the websites would have done would be stealing their data.

The second type of Phishing, popularly called Smishing, refers to the method in which the hacker would try to act as if they're your bank or any other service via email or SMS. It is very easy to spoof your email and make it seem legitimate. This is because the email core does not verify the names of the sender, and people can send an email with whatever email they wish in the sender's name.

So in other words, you could compose an email and put whatever you want in the "Sender" field, if you know how to do so. The hackers that use this technique usually know some information about you. They might, for example, know what bank you are a customer of. They would then send an email that would have your bank's official email address in the sender field and ask for information such as your card number and pin. That information is then used for fraud.

The third type of phishing is done over the phone and known as Vishing. There are two particular methods that are used in this. The first one involves spoofing the caller ID. This is very similar to email spoofing and allows the hacker to show their phone number as that of a legitimate institution. They use them combined with automated answering machines to steal information.

The second method used is easier if the victim is using a phone line. The hacker calls the victim and tells them of fraud and asks them to call their bank to confirm. They then pretend to hang up, playing flat tunes to indicate that the phone has been hung up. In reality, they're still on the other side of the line. The victim then calls the bank, and the hacker pretends to be the bank and obtains sensitive information that is later used for credit card fraud.

Cookie Theft

One of the more complicated ways of hacking into a system involves cookie theft. This is more complicated than most hacking mechanisms. Cookie theft involves stealing the cookies of a system. The cookies of a system are authenticating the information that is used to authenticate a person for website usage.

This can be done in a number of ways. Some of the ways include session fixation, Sidejacking, malware, and cross-site scripting. Session fixation refers to when the hacker sets the session to an id that is known to him. He does that by sending a specific link. When the user uses that link to log into a session, the hacker is able to steal the cookies. Sidejacking involves stealing the cookies using the Wi-Fi connection. Many websites do not use SSL certificates on their site, and any data sent can thus be sniffed from the Wi-Fi connection. Cross-site scripting involves tricking the victim's computer into running a script that makes the hacker obtain a copy of the cookies. Malware also digs into a system and retrieves the cookies for them.

Cookie logs the active sessions of a victim. This means that if a victim is signed in to a website, a cookie records that and lets them access the website continuously. Once a hacker has access to the cookie session, they are thus able to validate their own server or system and allow them to log in as well.

Using Wi-Fi for Hacking

While the Wi-Fi offers great accessibility for a user, it is also used as a window to hack into the system or a network. There are a number of ways that this can work. The first one involves a hacker targeting one particular person. They look at their schedules and find a way where they use the internet a lot, for example, at a cafe. They then set a fake WAP at the Cafe, naming it the same as the WAP that the victim typically uses. Once the victim is connected to their face Wi-Fi access point, they can read all the information that goes through it.

Another way is not to target a specific person but to target all the people in a specific area. So taking the Cafe example again, a hacker would simply set up a Wi-Fi access point in that location and let people connect to it. While people connect to it for free internet, the hacker can then read and access your data that you transmit through your Wi-Fi. This includes sensitive information, including passwords.

Trojan Horse

If you've read the Greek story of the infamous Trojan horse, you already know what you're dealing with here. The Trojans posed the horse as a gift and gave it to the Troy people. It was meant to show that the Trojans had given up, and Troy had won. In reality, though, the Trojan horse housed the army of Greece, which ambushed the city once the horse was pulled inside.

The virus functions in the same manner. It presents itself as software. Typically, Trojans tend to enter your system when you are trying to download software from unauthorized sites. The software isn't actual software and is just pretending to be one. Once you have installed the software, the Trojan can freely roam in your system.

The function of such a virus is to give control to the hacker by installing rootkits. By installing a Trojan in the system of the victim, the hacker can obtain control of the system of the victim. This means that they can do anything in the system of the victim, including accessing all data and deleting or transferring any data that they wish.

This makes the Trojan horse virus a particularly dangerous one, and antiviruses usually have dedicated functionalities to ensure that no Trojan goes undetected.

Keylogger

In a lot of ways, a keylogger replicates the behavior of a Trojan. It enters the system in a similar manner, but there are differences that we must take into account. The keylogger has a very simple function and is thus typically easier to develop than a Trojan horse.

What that means is that most hackers can easily use it by getting someone to download fake software.

The function of a keylogger is to log keystrokes. What that means is that it records all the keystrokes that a person makes on their system. This allows the hacker to access both personal information that a person may have typed out, as well as any passwords that a person inputs in the system. That way, he can easily gain access to the different accounts of the victim and use them for whatever purposes he wishes.

Keyloggers are now also able to carefully analyze the data that is input into them and dig out any passwords for the user, making it way easier to use them. They are thus a simple yet efficient way to hack into a system.

Drive-by Downloads

Drive-by downloads are websites that can force your browser to download a file when you visit them. These are powerful tools if someone is unable to convince other people to download malicious files on their own. Using this technique, the hacker can thus automatically get a file to download on a person's system and leave them vulnerable to Trojans and keyloggers, among other malware.

Social Engineering

One of the more modern and sophisticated techniques of hacking that is now commonly used requires very little technical knowledge. Social engineering is exactly what the name says. It's a method by which the hacker socially engineer their way into your system.

They do this by manipulating people on a human level and attempting to get confidential information out of them. The information that can be received includes things such as parent's names, credit card and other document related information, and other things. Once a person is able to access all of this data, they can steal the identity of the person to hack the system.

They do this by using the information that they have gained to prove that they are the owner of the user ID. Typically, forget password IDs can redirect you to security questions. These include Social Security Numbers and other such information. With the information that the hacker has now gained, they are easily able to cross the system and reset the password by assuming the identity of the person. This is a lengthy technique and often takes time since it would require the hacker to gain the trust of the victim.

Chapter Seven

How to Protect yourself from Hacking

Now that you know the different types of hacking that exist, it would be important to know how to protect yourself from them. Without having adequate protection and without knowing how you can ensure that you remain safe from these kinds of attacks, you would let yourself be very vulnerable to hacking. Let us explore the different ways in which hacking can occur and look into how you can keep yourself safe in case of such an attack.

Physical Hacking

Physical hacking is perhaps the easiest to save yourself from. Physical hacking requires that a person has access to the travel channels of your data or the storage servers. To ensure that that doesn't happen, you can do a number of things. The first would be to ensure that all your data is encrypted, and password protected. Numerous services offer you the services to encrypt your data, which would render it useless even if someone was able to steal them. Newer hard drives are also encryptable and can have passwords put over them to ensure that no one manages to enter them. However, it is important to remember that while encryption offers some form of safety, passwords on laptops, computers, and hard drives are typically not as great security. This is because brute force can be used on such a system, and would allow for a person to quickly dig into the data.

To secure a premise where your data is contained, a number of additional security measures can be taken. The first thing that you can do is to ensure that there are no vulnerabilities within the floor plan of the place where the confidential data is stored. While vents are necessary for heat sinks from the hard drives, they can be made much more secure by ensuring that better material is used for them. Alarms can also be placed inside the vents to alert the security in case someone tries to hack into them.

Similar measures can be taken in office spaces. A manager should ensure that different profiles are made for each of the employees so that the amount of data they are able to access is limited. This ensures that the lower-level employees that are not required to have access to any confidential data can be shut off from it. Managers should also ensure that the area where the computers and hard drives are kept is secure. There should be no unauthorized person in the place where the servers are kept. This can be done via the installation of CCTV and hiring some security.

In case of the absolute requirement of confidentiality, newer hard drives are available where the data can automatically be deleted in case someone tries to force their way into them. This ensures that no one can access your data and would render any and all attacks useless unless the person making the attacks is already aware of what the passwords are.

When it comes to hackers being able to tap into connecting lines between phones, things can get a lot tougher on the part of the company. It is usually not possible for a company to ensure that no one taps into the line. However, it is important to remember that landlines offer much higher security than the VOIP options. It is thus important to avoid unsafe connections such as VOIP when you are communicating some confidential information to another person. Moreover, the company should ensure that no one knows when they are making any confidential calls. If the times are not known to the hacker, they would naturally find it much harder to find the information they seek. Eavesdropping on lines all day long is very impractical for a hacker.

If you must absolutely use VOIP or other such vulnerable methods, we recommend using a VPN or a virtual private network. While a number of VPNs now offer free limited services, the services for large amounts of usage would cause you some money. However, they can save you from a lot of hassles. A VPN has a number of features that include identity masking as well as encryption. We will discuss these later.

Brute Force

Brute forcing passwords is one of the easiest things that a hacker can do to get access to your information. While there are a number of measures that internet service providers, as well as websites, have done to ensure that no one can brute force their way through the passwords, there are some cautions that you must take as well.

The first and frankly, the most important cautionary measure that you can take is to make your password difficult to guess. Surprisingly, a large number of people fail to do so. Millions of accounts are cracked into every year simply because the passwords that they choose are among a few of the following:

- Password

- Qwerty

- Their names

- Their pet's names

- Their crush's names

- Their favorite celebrities names

- Other similar easy to get information

This allows the hackers to quickly be able to get through the system and find your password.

Another thing that helps with brute force attacks is to have different passwords. To demonstrate how this helps, let us give you an example.

Consider that a hacker manages to find an application that does not require Captcha clearing before entering passwords again. In that case, they would be able to hack through and get your password on that particular application. Most people keep similar passwords on most applications, and hackers are aware of that. If you do the same, the hacker would now also be able to access anything and everything from your internet banking application to your Facebook account.

If you keep different passwords for all applications, though, you would be able to keep your other accounts safe. There are many accounts that allow you to enter the password a limited number of times, and they would thus be safe. If it is a hassle to remember a large number of difficult passwords, then you can find a number of applications to help you both find strong passwords as well as to keep them safe and allow you to log in on devices that are already approved automatically.

Phishing

Phishing is one of the easiest ways in which a hacker can access your information. It is luckily also the method that you can easily evade with a little common sense and help. To understand how to ensure that no information is given out using phishing, we have to look into each type of phishing individually.

The first type of phishing comes in the form of websites that are made to replicate other websites that you typically use. These are generally very easy to unmask. First off, you need to ensure that any website that you are linked to via an advertisement or a message is legitimate. For that, you can check the certificate of a site. If a website has an HTTP instead of HTTPS at the start, it is typically a high-risk site, and you should be careful navigating over it. You should ideally carefully read the link to ensure that you are on the right site. There are a number of characters that can easily be confused, including the O and 0, and 1 and I, so you should pay careful attention to those.

If you have any form of doubt about the validity of the site that is asking you for the password, there is a simple procedure. You can enter an incorrect username and passwords. Phishing sites do not carry out any validation and simply store the information. Thus it would accept any and all username and passwords that you throw at it. That is an obvious indication of a site being made for Phishing.

The second kind of Phishing comes in the form of emails and SMS. These, although seemingly valid, are typically spoofed. Luckily, the procedure to find out if an email is spoofed is not too difficult. All you have to do is click reply to the email. When you are trying to reply to an email, it is going to be sent to the person that sent the email in the first place, and not to the spoofed address that it showed that the email came from. Thus by clicking a reply, you can easily find out who the email that you will be sending is going to and avoid giving out information if it's anyone not trustable.

Another important thing to remember is never to share sensitive information over email. Companies would never ask you to email them your password or any other similar information, so be wary of such requests!

The third type of Phishing comes as the voiced variant. There are two ways in which that occurs. The first method uses call spoofing. It is important to ensure that you never enter your information on calls that require you to enter them. Your banks would never ask for such information from you via call.

The second type is a scam where the caller pretends to hang up. It is best practice to put the phone down and ensure that the power line is cut before moving on to call the bank. That ensures that you are safe, and the call was actually held up, and no one is on the other side, trying to listen to your confidential information.

With these simple practices, you can ensure that you are never a victim of phishing attacks and are able to keep yourself safe. These steps are very simple and can save you from a lot of hassles!

Cookie Theft

Your cookies are a piece of information that you should never let hacker access. If a hacker can access your cookies, they can be authorized to enter your accounts and do as they will. That is why you have to ensure that they are unable to get to your cookies in any way.

We previously discussed four different methods in which a hacker can access your cookies. We will now look at how you can save yourself from each one of them.

The first method is session fixation and needs you to click a link to open a session with a particular ID. To ensure that you are not led to a session created to steal your cookies, it is important that you do not use the links that are emailed to you from fishy-looking email addresses. Even legit email addresses should be confirmed by clicking a reply, as we have already mentioned before. These measures ensure that you are never at risk of having a fixated session again.

Sidejacking involves stealing cookies via the Wi-Fi network. That means that both you and the hacker have to be on the same Wi-Fi network. It is thus recommended for you to keep your Wi-Fi password protected. In case of you being in a public place, you should ensure that any websites that you visit are encrypted. When the websites have SSL or TLS certifications, a hacker would be unable to access the information of the session and fail to steal the cookies.

This can be done in a number of ways. Some of the ways include session fixation, sidejacking, malware, and cross-site scripting. Session fixation refers to when the hacker sets the session to an id that is known to him. He does that by sending a specific link. When the user uses that link to log into a session, the hacker is able to steal the cookies. Sidejacking involves stealing the cookies using the Wi-Fi connection. Many websites do not use SSL certificates on their site, and any data sent can thus be sniffed from the Wi-Fi connection. Cross-site scripting involves tricking the victim's computer into running a script that makes the hacker obtain a copy of the cookies. Malware also digs into a system and retrieves the cookies for them. You can use certain applications that force the encryption to ensure that you are always safe.

The third method that we discussed was the installation of malware. Malware cannot enter your system until and unless you allow for your system to download it. You should ensure that you do not download anything from fishy sites and that you have a good antivirus available on your system for your protection.

The last kind of cookie stealing is done by running scripts on the system of the victim. The scripts again, need to be executed by the victim. Trickery is often used for that purpose. Many websites would offer you scripts that they would claim would activate your windows or give you an adobe license. All the scripts do is steal your cookies and send them to the hacker. To ensure this doesn't happen to you, don't download untrusted software and never run scripts that you find on unreliable sources on the internet. If a script sounds too good to be true, it most probably is!

Wi-Fi-Based Hacking

Wi-Fi-based hacking can be scary. However, it is also very easy to ensure that you don't become a victim in this case. The first type of Wi-Fi-based hacking is where a person is specifically targeted. For that to happen, the hacker would have to chase you physically. That means that you should know that someone has been keeping tabs on you if you're simply a little aware of your surroundings. If you go to the same Cafe to use your internet at all times and find someone always chasing behind you, then you already know that there is something problematic. You can consider changing Cafes or not logging into an active session in their presence.

The second kind of hacking occurs when someone makes their own WAP and gives out free internet to steal data. A number of remedies are available to you in that case. The easiest one is to never log in to any places using the Wi-Fi that you can't trust, as well as to never send out any confidential information using it. However, that is not the best solution since you might need to connect to Wi-Fi for some reason.

Another better resource is available in the form of a VPN. A VPN, aka a virtual private network, ensures that there is another security layer between you and the hacker, and ensures that they are not able to tap into your data.

Trojan Horse

A Trojan horse is pretty similar to any other malware, and the best way to deal with them comes in the form of simple solutions that are applicable to all other such software.

The first way to deal with Trojans comes in the form of precautionary measures. These measures are made to ensure that the Trojan does not enter your system in the first place. These include measures such as ensuring that you never download software from places that you don't trust. Most third party downloading sites are infected with malware and should be avoided at all costs.

The second important thing to note is that you should not download attachments from emails that you do not trust. If someone has emailed you a random file with no explanation, you should avoid it by all means and not download it, for it may contain malware.

If malware has already entered your system, you need to ensure that it is unable to act and take control. It is especially dangerous once it has accessed your BIOS using a rootkit, so immediate action must be taken. For that, you should, first of all, ensure that you are already using a reputable antivirus. Antiviruses typically already have lists of known Trojans and can easily locate as well as quarantine them.

Another important tool is a sandbox. In case of having to download something that you do not trust, it is recommended that you do so in the sandbox. A sandbox is a virtual container within your system in which you can download any files and test them. If they display abnormal behavior, only the sandbox would be infected and can be deleted. If they are safe, you can then download them directly to your system.

If you are already infected by a Trojan, you should download an anti-malware software such as Malwarebytes to ensure that you can remove it from your system. If the malware has dug into your BIOS as well, you should always perform a BIOS reset to ensure that any rootkits are removed from your system completely.

Keylogger

A keylogger can be a lethal hacking tool. Fortunately, it has its own downs. Any keylogger must be able to transmit data back to the hacker for it to work. That means that there is a strong chance that any firewall would detect the keylogger at work and alert you about it. It is thus important to ensure that your firewall is on at all times to prevent keylogger-based attacks on your system.

A keylogger typically behaves like malware, so the same precautions as a trojan horse apply. You shouldn't download malicious and unknown content, and you should keep your system protected by using a strong antivirus.

For both keyloggers and trojans, one thing that would help is to update your system constantly. With system updates, you will usually find many of the older exploits are closed down, and the defense is much better, ensuring that your system is kept safe from prying eyes of the hacker.

Drive-by Downloads

Drive-by downloads enable the downloading of malware into your system. There are a number of ways in which you can prevent that from happening.

The first thing that you should consider is to disable auto-downloading options. Most browsers are equipped with an optional turning off of automatic downloads. Any download requests thrown by the website would thus not be processed, and anything that you don't download won't be downloaded.

It is also important to not click links you are sent by a third party or ad sources unless you trust them. The links might often redirect to sites that are made to force downloads of malware.

Having a decent defense system, including a strong antivirus as well as a firewall, can also help. These would immediately quarantine any threat even if it were to be downloaded. It is also helpful to remember that most applications require permission before running. If anything is downloaded automatically, delete it instead of running the script!

Social Engineering

Social engineering is a tricky hacking technique. It is consequently also tricky to avoid. Luckily, with a few precautions, you can generally ensure that you are not a victim of social engineering.

The first thing that you have to remember when it comes to social engineering is to keep your security question and answer safe. Make the answer unique and never tell anyone what it is. Questions like "What's your mother's name" are too easily guessable and should either be avoided completely or should have unique and untrue answers so that no one can engineer their way into your system.

If a sketchy person seems to be taking an unusual interest in particular information that can directly be connected to your bank account, it is usually presumable that the person has malicious intent. You should ensure that no answers are given to such a person, and your personal information remains safe and personal.

Many websites now allow you to set up two-factor authentication and other methods of accessing your information to ensure that you are not made a target of social engineering. You should always enable any such options for added security. It is also usually helpful to have a valid phone number or email address where password reset links can be set. If those exist, most sites will not rely on having to second-guess your identity, potentially letting someone steal it along the way.

You should also ensure that you are aware of the security protocols of your bank. You can normally set limits, transactions above, which would be confirmed from you via the number you provided to the bank. This ensures that no one can pretend to be you and rob you of your money.

Chapter Eight

Cybersecurity and How it Saves you from being Hacked

Now that we have gone over some of the basics of hacking and how to prevent yourself from them, it is important to see how systems, as well as websites and applications, aim to save both you and them from hacking. To dig deeper into that information, we have to look at the different ways in which cybersecurity works.

What is Cybersecurity?

Cybersecurity refers to the practice that is used to protect programs, networks, and users from digital or cyber-attacks. They can operate in a number of ways, but the end goal remains the same: to keep the data safe and secure and to ensure that no one can malign, steal, or otherwise destroy it.

We will now explore the different countermeasures that are available against a cyber-attack and how they can help a network evade any form of attack.

Countermeasures by Design

Countermeasures are designed to mean that a system is made to ensure that the maximum amount of security is available to the network and its users. The design elements that can help with security offer a number of features.

One of the main design features to ensure high security is the principle of least privilege. This is a very simple mechanism and offers any user only the minimum authority within a system, as is needed by them. This ensures that even if a hacker assumes the role of anyone within a network, they would be unable to do much and would not be able to access data, alter it, or delete it.

Other design mechanisms that can enhance security include defense in depth. This refers to systems where you need to breach more than one aspect of the system to be able to penetrate it. So, for example, a system might need authorization from both user 1 and user 2 to allow access to anyone to the sensitive data. This design means that the hacker has to hack through multiple security systems, and makes it much harder for a hacker to be able to gain control.

Another important design measure comes in the form of audit trails, which ensures that if any vulnerability is detected, either through black hat hacking attacks or otherwise, it is promptly dealt with, and the system is not left vulnerable in the end. This keeps the system safe from further attacks down the line.

Security Architecture

This form of countermeasure aims to design the system in a way that makes hacking difficult. This is mostly a design-based system but rather deals with how various entities within a network interact with each other. By limiting the dependence of a system on other systems, we can ensure that the hacker does not gain control of the whole system even if he enters a part of it.

Another important role of security architecture is to ensure that any and all entries and vulnerabilities are covered by the security systems in place. It thus dictates where the security measures are placed to ensure that no vulnerabilities remain.

System Penetration Testing

An important way of checking the security design, architecture, and strength of your system is to do a system penetration testing. A penetration testing, which is also popularly known as pen testing is a way of accessing the vulnerabilities within a system to ensure that all of them are closed. There are a number of ways in which a system can conduct penetration testing to ensure that there are no vulnerabilities within the system

If a company, system, or network does not have the resources to hire themselves a hacker, they can usually use software that is already available to conduct such tests. These include tools like MetaSpoilt that we have already discussed. These tools have distinct functions. When they are made to test a network, they will find out all the vulnerabilities. Many tools also exist that can both exploit these vulnerabilities to assess the damage to the system that would occur in case of an attack, as well as provide solutions to these damages to ensure that they do not occur in the future.

For the best service, though, the automated tools are left far behind. The persons that one should refer to for the best analysis are the white hat hackers. White hat hackers are usually skilled in penetrating a system and can quickly point out flaws that would not have been pointed out by any other traditional script. However, they can be expensive to hire.

When a white hat hacker is hired, you can make them test the system in two ways. The first type is black box hacking and would mean that the hacker is not told any facts about the network. This is a useful method if you also wish to see how easy it is to find information about your network. Having accessed the information, the hacker would then write scripts to find vulnerabilities, in a much more efficient way than the pre-written scripts could have done. These vulnerabilities are then reported back to the person that hired the white hat hacker to ensure that they can be closed. Black box testing is a good way to see the practical security level that your system holds.

Another type of white hat hacking can be employed. This type revolves around a white box methodology. What that means is that the hacker is already told all the information that he needs to know about the network, and the code and system are transparent before him. This is especially beneficial when you want an in-depth penetration testing since, with the information that the hacker would already have, he can dig much deeper into the vulnerabilities. Most companies would use a mixture of white box and black box based white hat hacking to ensure that the hacker is both able to find the issues in-depth and able to show a realistic strength value of the system.

Elite groups of hackers are usually able to write scripts that other hackers cannot hope to reproduce. They are thus typically paid way higher, and companies tend to employee them to find any flaws where the business model requires high network security. Such models can include government websites as well as websites of cloud storage apps.

If cost is an issue to you and you feel that your system is already impenetrable, a new form of white hat hacking contracts is now becoming popular. These are performance-based. A forum of hackers is offered a bounty for being able to hack into the system of the company. If no hacker succeeds, you already know your system is strong enough. If someone does, you need to spend the money only in that case. This helps save money if you're already sure of your security.

Two-Factor Authentication

One of the prime ways to ensure that no one is easily able to access the system is to use two-factor authentication. That means that you need two distinct pieces of information to access the data. These typically include one pin or password, and one hardware or biological trait. Typical systems can combine pins with thumbprint scans. Having a system that is based on these traits can mean that it is much more secure. Fingerprints are hard to replicate and typically require access to the victim. Similarly, for any cards using NFC to allow access to a system, the victim's card must be stolen. In such a case, a victim can usually quickly inform the system about a stolen card and thus ensure that the system is not compromised using it. Having a two-factor authentication can thus make your system much more secure, and make penetration much more difficult.

Data Security: Encryption, Protocols, Packets, and Transmission

Data has to travel around a lot. That leaves data very vulnerable. If data is sent through a simple wire with nothing to hide it, hackers can simply dig right into it. That is where the data security features come in. There are a number of ways in which data is protected. We will explore each of them in detail to see how your data manages to travel from one place to another safely.

If your data is traveling in the form of simple radio waves or through copper lines, anyone with the right software can read the data and thus be able to get your information. Radio waves are particularly unsafe since you don't need to find a line to tap into physically, and the risk of being caught is thus mitigated. Newer technologies now rely on fiber optics, which is more secure. This is because when someone tries to tap into a fiber optic, it will break the glass and possibly trigger alarms. This means that data that travels through that channel is typically much more secure.

However, most of the systems, especially WAN and remote areas, continue to use radio waves or copper-based wires. Fiber optic is also not impenetrable in any way. That is why data transmission is risky.

To help mitigate the risk, a number of ways are used. These include encryption and packet-based transmissions. We will look into both of them in detail.

Encryption means that data is distorted so that it is not readable. The earliest forms of encryption include the easier Caesar cipher, more popularly known as the shift cipher. The protocol is basically simple. The data in such a cipher is simply encrypted by using a shift. Thus a is transmitted as b, b is transmitted as c, and so on so forth. Of course, given the computing power of today's world, such algorithms are obsolete. We now have more reliable solutions to ensure our security.

There are two basic types of encryption. The first type is symmetric encryption. Data that has been encrypted using this form of encryption can only be decrypted by using the same key that encrypted it. This means that the key has to be transferred as well. This can lead to a security risk since hackers can ultimately intercept the key as well. However, if the key is transmitted in a secure manner, no significant concerns should arise.

Data is typically transmitted as packets. This means that not all the data is channeled at once, but data is rather divided up into small packets that are sent simultaneously or one by one, through a network. All of these packets then combine at the end receiver to make a complete data set, which can be decrypted using the key that was transported by any means. If you are using symmetric encryption, it is thus very important to ensure that the key is kept safe.

In using asymmetric encryption, the data is encrypted using a public key and decrypted using an individual private key. Since the key does not have to be shared, it is typically thought to be more secure. Nonetheless, you have to keep the key safe and ensure that no one can assume your identity or steal your cookies for that to work. Websites that use asymmetric methods of data encryptions typically have the HTTPS tag and have SSL technology, which ensures that any information that you enter on those sites is kept secure. You shouldn't enter sensitive information on websites that lack those protocols.

There are various algorithms that are used within encryptions that are important to know if you wish to keep your data safe. The earlier algorithms include the DES and triple-DES that were found to eventually become vulnerable as technology caught on and was able to brute force the algorithms. Newer algorithms such as the AES can make your data virtually unhackable. Using the current technology, AES 256 encryption would take billions of years to crack!

Protocols define how the algorithms should be utilized, and allow for secure key exchange among other functions. The protocols are thus an important part of the process since they allow for the data to be readable to the intended user.

So to summarize, while data can still be tapped into, it is often kept in the form of cryptic algorithms that can only be decrypted using keys that are transferred using secure protocols such as SSL. As long as a system sticks to the protocols, encrypts the data, and uses protocols like SSL to keep their data secure, the system itself cannot be brute-forced, and that means that vulnerabilities in terms of data in transit are minimalized.

Encryption is also possible on data at a resting stage, and with those, you can similarly ensure that the data cannot be accessed. However, the decryption keys are usually kept behind simple passwords that can be brute-forced. To ensure that brute force attacks do not succeed, a network can use a number of smart security designing that we will next explore.

Preventing Brute Force Attacks

Brute force attacks can both be used to hack into a system that stores data at rest, as well as to access the data of the users of the network by finding their passwords. With there being a very limited selection of passwords that people typically opt for, and computing being super powerful now, it is hard to prevent an attack that focuses on brute force. Luckily, with a few changes in design, this can be rendered useless.

The important thing to remember here is that a brute force attack aims to mainly get access to the data by having an infinite number of tries at guessing the password. Systems have now been designed to restrict the number of tries that a person can have at guessing. Most online log-in applications would either send ReCaptcha tests that the brute force algorithm would be unable to solve and thus stop it, or would simply lock the account down after a number of tries. Doing this, they are able to ensure that the brute force mechanism cannot continue to dig into the system. This is an important aspect of security since by adding this feature, you can ensure that even if someone manages to reach your key and has to guess a password simply, they would be unable to do so quickly.

To make things even more secure, logs can be taken of attempts at logging in to a system. The logs will show when someone tried to log into a system and the passwords that were input. This means that the admin can be altered about a brute force attack, and measures can be taken to ensure that care is taken of it.

By using this measure, a network can ensure that no one is able to gain unauthorized access by way of guessing passwords. It is also a helpful feature to include in case of a website having web portals, and many applications such as Gmail and Dell do make extensive use of it to ensure that the accounts of individuals registered for their services are not compromised.

Firewall

A firewall is an underrated aspect of network security. In simple terms, a firewall monitors all incoming as well as outgoing traffic and governs it via specified rules. This is very important since otherwise, people can simply send packets of malware to your system.

A firewall is a wall between your network and the outside world. It inspects all incoming data packets and reads the protocols, including FTP, HTTP, and DNS. It then uses the rules that are predetermined to decide if a packet should be allowed into the system or not. Similarly, it also inspects packets going out of the system. This is useful since, in case of a hacker using scripts to gain data or logging your keystrokes and trying to access them, the firewall can inspect the packets and identify there being something wrong, and thus block transmissions.

Given the function of a firewall, it is absolutely crucial for a system to have a good firewall. Firewalls now come with greater functionalities, and features and customizations are pretty simple and straightforward. Companies that require the ultimate security solutions could customize a firewall to their needs and ensure that no data is transmitted in or out of the system without proper authorization.

A firewall is the first defense that a system has, and can be useful by preventing malware from getting into the system and preventing system data from flowing out. A strong firewall is thus protection we should all consider getting.

Anti-Virus and Anti-Malware Software

Anti-virus and anti-malware software typically form a secondary line of defense. The function is simple. They scan the system and try and find any programs that are known for being problematic. Most anti-viruses have huge repositories of codes and can easily identify viruses and trojans by matching them with the codes of other known threats.

The threats are then alerted to the system admin, who can then decide to quarantine or remove the threat. Such removal ensures that the threat is no longer active. They can identify a number of threats, including trojans, rootkits, spam and scams, phishing, and DDoS.

Given the versatility of this software, it is absolutely essential for anyone that works with sensitive data to get one of the premium plans of a reputable anti-virus. By doing so, not only would they be able to identify any trojans or other malware, but they would also be kept safe from phishing attacks and other such hacking methods.

Internet of Things: The Unpatched Cybersecurity Threat

One of the prime things that can cause a system threat is via the internet of things. The internet of things refers to any and all things that require internet or network access to work. These include a number of things, including modern homes, garage doors, cars, printers, refrigerators, and whatnot. With a large number of manufacturers now letting you control your electronics using your cell phone, the internet of things becomes all the more important.

Sadly, we see that vendors typically give very little emphasis to this industry in terms of cybersecurity, and simple patches that would seal vulnerabilities are never made. This means that everything from your printer to your garage door is hackable and can be hacked with ease.

Given the digital world that we are moving to, it is high time for manufacturers to place more emphasis on the security of such systems and to ensure that they are made as secure as the other systems are. Ultimately, all networks should be made secure so that hackers can no longer be a menace, and without a focus on the internet of things, we can expect to continue to see successful cyber-attacks.

How are Cybersecurity Tools used to Secure your Wi-Fi Connection?

Wi-Fi connections are typically very vulnerable. If you are going to be using a public router, in a hacker's eye, you're an easy target. Luckily, with newer system updates, many operating systems include inbuilt protection against such attacks.

Taking the example of windows, when you connect to a network, a system will typically ask you if the network is public or private. In case of you being on a public network, windows will automatically hide your device and make it undiscoverable. This ensures that you are kept safe, even where you are connected to a public network. It is important to be still wary, though, since the network admin can still see the information that you transmit, and WAP attacks are commonplace. That is where a VPN comes in. Let's explore a VPN in more detail.

Virtual Private Network

A VPN or a virtual private network allows you to transmit data using a public network as if you were transmitting it using a private network. There are a number of ways that this is achieved, and we will look into some of them.

To start with, a VPN masks your identity and shows a different IP address. This is typically done by masking your IP with another IP that belongs to the VPN server. This means that anyone that intercepts the data will not know where the data came from, and would rather believe it to have come from a virtual IP address that the VPN sets for you.

Secondly, VPN tunnels past the public servers. This means that the data that is sent through the VPN is delivered through packets. Each of those packets has a protocol and is duly encrypted. The encrypted packets cannot be decrypted in the public network, and would only allow the intended recipient with the key to decrypt them. Thus even where the WAP hacker manages to get a hold of the packages, he would be able to find little use for them. VPN thus ensures that you get the maximum security, and your data is kept safe. It is very important for a firm to use VPNs if they are transmitting highly sensitive data over Wi-Fi since Wi-Fi can be hacked into and allow for someone to sniff the data. That is why VPN, along with other cybersecurity methodologies, becomes an important part of any defense arsenal against cyber-attacks.

Conclusion

Now that we have analyzed all the ways that hacking occurs and the tools that hackers may use to enter a system, as well as mentioned the ways in which you can ensure that you remain safe from hacking, we hope that you have found the answers to all the burning questions that you had.

A few short takeaways include that your data is very vulnerable, and everyone, even newbies, can crack into it unless you take steps to secure it. This is especially true for networks since more people tend to want to break into networks. That is why one should always ensure that their network is able to past the penetration tests and has an adequate design. This would ensure that the data of both the network and the customers are kept safe.

There are a large number of ways in which you can protect yourself, and the best combination for you depends on your individual needs. A website that uses no Wi-Fi-based communication networks in public, for example, would not need a VPN tunneling based security system. Similarly, any network that blocks out all external data and takes no inputs would have no use of a firewall.

Whatever your business model or product may be, irrespective of if you're a simple social media user, a small company, or a large network, hacking is a menace to anyone connected to the internet. That doesn't mean that it has to be that way. Hacking can be fought against in simple steps that we highlighted in this book, and by using them, you can ensure that your data and identity are never compromised again.

Remember, prevention is better than cure. Once a hacker has your data, it is really hard to be able to retrieve it and get it deleted from the internet. You should thus ensure that you follow the guidelines that are made to ensure that your accounts do not get hacked, and you should ensure that your network has a proper cybersecurity plan that it uses to protect itself against any such attacks. We hope that this book was helpful to you in achieving your ultimate hacker-free dreams and that you will now surf the internet safer (or make a career out of ethical hacking!)

Made in the USA
Las Vegas, NV
08 February 2024

85493461R00038